TECH **TITANS**

MICROSOFT

BY LAURA LANE

CONTENT CONSULTANT

Anthony Rotolo
Media Scholar, Speaker, and Consultant

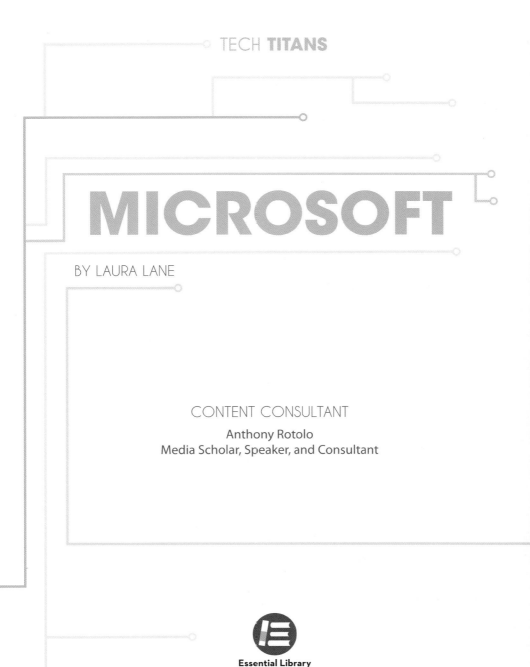

Essential Library

An Imprint of Abdo Publishing | abdobooks.com

ABDOBOOKS.COM

Published by Abdo Publishing, a division of ABDO, PO Box 398166, Minneapolis, Minnesota 55439. Copyright © 2019 by Abdo Consulting Group, Inc. International copyrights reserved in all countries. No part of this book may be reproduced in any form without written permission from the publisher. Essential Library™ is a trademark and logo of Abdo Publishing.

Printed in the United States of America, North Mankato, Minnesota.
082018
012019

THIS BOOK CONTAINS RECYCLED MATERIALS

Cover Photo: Mark Kauzlarich/Bloomberg/Getty Images
Interior Photos: Freek van den Bergh/ANP/Newscom, 4–5; Richard Drew/AP Images, 6; Mike Blake/Reuters/Newscom, 13; Red Line Editorial, 15, 95, 97; Ron Wurzer/Getty Images News/Getty Images, 16–17; Doug Wilson/Corbis Historical/Getty Images, 20; Jose Luis Magana/AP Images, 23; Keith Beaty/Toronto Star/Getty Images, 26–27; John Lok/Seattle Times/MCT/Newscom, 31; SSPL/Getty Images, 33; Deborah Feingold/Corbis Historica/Getty Images, 36–37; David Cooper/Toronto Star/Getty Images, 41; Claudio Cruz/AP Images, 43; Shutterstock Images, 46, 91; Dwayne Newton/AP Images, 48–49; AP Images, 52; Doug Mills/AP Images, 56; Ben Margot/AP Images, 59; Jeff Christensen/Hulton Archive/Getty Images, 62–63; Mario Tama/Getty Images Entertainment/Getty Images, 64; Chris Hondros/Hulton Archive/Getty Images, 70–71; Paul Sakuma/AP Images, 74; Jeff Christensen/Sipa/Newscom, 76; Eric Risberg/AP Images, 78; Pieter Beens/Shutterstock Images, 80–81; Elaine Thompson/AP Images, 86; Rafiq Maqbool/AP Images, 88–89

Editor: Arnold Ringstad
Series Designer: Laura Polzin

Library of Congress Control Number: 2018948250

Publisher's Cataloging-in-Publication Data

Names: Lane, Laura, author.
Title: Microsoft / by Laura Lane.
Description: Minneapolis, Minnesota : Abdo Publishing, 2019 | Series: Tech titans | Includes online resources and index.
Identifiers: ISBN 9781532116896 (lib. bdg.) | ISBN 9781532159732 (ebook)
Subjects: LCSH: Microsoft Corporation--Juvenile literature. | Computer software--Juvenile literature. | Computers--Juvenile literature. | Technology--Juvenile literature.
Classification: DDC 338.470040--dc23

CONTENTS

CHAPTER ONE

PIONEERING MIXED-REALITY TECHNOLOGY

The first time Mark Griswold, a professor at Case Western Reserve University, strapped Microsoft's HoloLens around his head, the experience was breathtaking. "I immediately knew my world had changed that day," he later said in a *National Geographic* article.[1]

When he put on the HoloLens, Griswold saw a vivid, three-dimensional hologram of the surface of Mars projected over his view of the real world. It was as if Griswold were standing on top of a mountain on the Red Planet itself. A National Aeronautics and Space Administration (NASA) scientist was standing next to him, and the two men could chat and interact together. But the scientist was a holographic image too.

Microsoft's HoloLens packs sophisticated computing and display technology into a compact headset.

The HoloLens technology beamed in the scientist from a different location.

SETTING THE STANDARD

The HoloLens offers an intriguing glimpse into the future of computing. It is just one example of how Microsoft is at the forefront of developing new and advanced computer technologies. In its more than 40-year history, the company has made a name for itself by creating technologies that change the way people live and work. In its early years, Microsoft's creation of the Windows operating system and its Office software set industry standards and helped popularize the use of personal computers in homes and businesses around the world.

Microsoft's Windows operating system is the company's best-known and most widely used product.

Today, the extraordinary popularity and dominance of Microsoft's products continues. By 2017, its Windows 10 operating system was active on more than 500 million devices around the world. More than 100 million people used Microsoft's Office 365 software at work, whereas 27 million consumers used Office 365 at home. In gaming, more than 53 million members were active on Xbox Live, the company's online gaming service.[2]

MICROSOFT BY THE NUMBERS

In 2017, Microsoft reported $89.5 billion in revenue. The company employed 128,290 people in March 2018. Of those employees, 75,910 lived in the United States. In the state of Washington alone, Microsoft had 47,679 employees.[3]

Devices such as the HoloLens capture people's imagination about where computers will take them in the future. Microsoft is a pioneer in the field of mixed-reality technology. It announced the development of the HoloLens in 2015. The device became available to developers and commercial partners in the United States and Canada in 2016. Later that year, it became available in other countries, too, including Australia, France, Germany, Ireland, New Zealand, and the United Kingdom. With a $3,000 price tag, this early version of the HoloLens was intended for serious developers and commercial partners rather than everyday consumers.[4]

A GROUNDBREAKING DEVICE

The HoloLens is the world's first self-contained holographic computer. It is a circular headset that sits on top of the user's head like a crown. There are two clear lenses over the user's eyes. The device doesn't need a separate computer, smartphone, or tablet to work.

The HoloLens is different from a virtual reality headset. With a virtual reality headset, the device blocks out the real world and the user is immersed in a completely different world. The HoloLens is called a mixed-reality or augmented-reality headset because users can see both the holographic images and their real physical environment at the same time. In essence, holographic images are layered on top of a user's surroundings. For example, a promotional video from Microsoft showed the HoloLens creating holograms of *Minecraft* environments on top of a kitchen table.

While wearing the HoloLens, the user has access to Microsoft's Edge web browser, Skype video conferencing, and a variety of other applications. The applications appear as floating windows before the user's eyes. Users of the HoloLens can resize and reposition the holographic images. They can walk around the three-dimensional objects and look at the images from any angle.

TEACHING ANATOMY IN THREE DIMENSIONS

Griswold, a professor of radiology, had been invited to a demonstration of the HoloLens at Microsoft's top-secret testing facility in 2014. After trying out the HoloLens, he realized this new technology could revolutionize the way medical students learn human anatomy. Case Western Reserve University and the Cleveland Clinic were planning to build a state-of-the-art health sciences center and wanted to incorporate the latest technological advances. Griswold

A REVIEW OF MICROSOFT'S HOLOLENS

In 2016, Will Greenwald, a senior analyst at *PCMag*, tried out the HoloLens and wrote a review of the device. Greenwald found the HoloLens "surprisingly intuitive and fleshed out for development hardware." He said the holograms were bright and clear and there was an interesting selection of software available on the device. However, he also found the HoloLens uncomfortable to wear for long periods and felt silly making gestures while using it. He said the holograms appeared only in a small section of his vision. Greenwald summarized that the HoloLens "is a well-executed and tempting look at how we might use computers years in the future."[5]

had been searching for a new way to use technology to teach students anatomy. Traditionally, medical students dissect cadavers to learn about the body, but anatomy laboratories filled with cadavers are expensive to maintain and use harsh chemicals.

The HoloLens pointed to a better way. Medical students could strap the devices onto their heads and view three-dimensional images of the human body's organs and systems. The technology allows students to walk around and examine the body's parts from different angles. For example, when a student dons the HoloLens to see a holographic heart, he or she can move parts of the heart in and out, turn the heart around, and see the blood pumping.

Satyam Ghodasara had already taken a traditional anatomy class at Case Western Reserve, but it wasn't until he saw a holographic heart using the HoloLens that he fully saw the aortic valve as separate from the other parts of the heart. "There's the aortic valve," he exclaimed. "Now I understand."[6]

In 2016, at Microsoft's annual Build conference in San Francisco, California, a three-dimensional holographic image of Griswold's head and hand appeared before a packed auditorium. Griswold himself was across the country in Cleveland, Ohio. Griswold's holographic image guided the audience through an examination of the white matter tracts of the brain, fibers that act as superhighways by allowing messages to travel from one part of the brain to another. "This is our new system," Griswold said, "which allows me to teach and interact with you, even though I'm not there. . . . This is really changing what it means to be 'in class.'"[7]

Case Western Reserve planned to open an anatomy lab designed with the help of the HoloLens, and students will use a curriculum built around the HoloLens. Griswold believes the potential uses of the HoloLens in education are limitless. "I don't see a class on campus that won't be affected by the technology," he said.[8] Griswold is confident that in time, the HoloLens will be as common in students' backpacks as laptops and smartphones.

THE HOLOANATOMY APP

In partnership with Microsoft and the Cleveland Clinic, Griswold led a team at Case Western Reserve that developed HoloAnatomy, the first third-party app available for the HoloLens. Medical students who previously learned human anatomy by dissecting cadavers tested the HoloAnatomy app. Eighty-five percent of the more than three dozen students participating in the study said they learned something new with the HoloLens.[9]

SCIENTISTS "WORK ON MARS"

Like the team at Case Western Reserve, scientists at NASA's Jet Propulsion Laboratory (JPL) in California recognized how the HoloLens could help them. In their case, the device could assist in studying the planet Mars. In 2015, researchers at JPL partnered with Microsoft to develop software for the HoloLens called OnSight. With OnSight, scientists can put on a mixed-reality headset and walk around Mars's surface from their offices on Earth. The three-dimensional holographic images of Mars come from data collected by the *Curiosity* rover.

The rover landed on Mars in August 2012. It is a robotic vehicle that travels over Mars's surface and collects samples of Martian rocks and soil. The rover is equipped with advanced instruments for scientific study. Its onboard laboratory can analyze soil and rock samples, which can tell scientists about the planet's climate and geology. Part of the rover's mission is to determine whether Mars has ever been capable of supporting microbes.

Before the HoloLens technology, scientists had to study the rover's data from Mars on a computer screen. Now, they can strap on a HoloLens and experience

Scientists can get a new perspective on Mars using HoloLens headsets.

what it would be like to actually walk on the planet's rocky surface, closely examining the landscape from many different angles. "This tool gives them the ability to explore the rover's surroundings much as an Earth geologist would do field work here on our planet," said Jeff Norris, JPL's OnSight project manager.[10]

NASA also partnered with Microsoft on Project Sidekick. The goal of Project Sidekick was to explore how mixed-reality headsets such as the HoloLens could help astronauts do repairs and other operations on the International Space Station. American astronaut Scott Kelly tested the HoloLens during his time on the International Space Station and said the HoloLens helped him communicate with Mission Control on Earth when he was performing complex tasks in orbit. The ground crew could also see what Kelly was viewing through the HoloLens. "I could say, 'Hey, is this the bolt or connector you're talking about?' And the person [at Mission Control] could just write an arrow in [my] field of view," Kelly said.[11]

THE MODERN MICROSOFT

Today, Microsoft explains that its mission is to empower every person and every organization on the planet to achieve more. The company believes people will experience computing in a more multisensory way that involves voices, gestures, and even the objects a user looks at. The HoloLens is an example of this multisensory experience.

Along with devices such as HoloLens, Microsoft is investing deeply in new artificial intelligence technologies. In 2016, the company announced the formation of its Artificial Intelligence and Research Group. In addition to adding

FARMERS USE MICROSOFT'S CLOUD SERVICES

In his letter to shareholders in 2017, Satya Nadella, Microsoft's chief executive officer (CEO), described how food company Land O' Lakes is using Microsoft Azure to help its farmers make the best planting decisions. Through this initiative, farmers can access real-time weather information, agronomic research, and satellite data.

MICROSOFT'S REVENUES BY DIVISION, 2017[12]

(In millions)

REVENUE	2017
Productivity and Business Processes Microsoft's Productivity and Business Processes segment includes such products as Microsoft Office, Skype, and LinkedIn.	$30,444
Intelligent Cloud The Intelligent Cloud segment includes the company's programs and services that run on servers.	$27,440
More Personal Computing The More Personal Computing segment includes Windows, Xbox, and hardware.	$38,773
Corporate and Other The Corporate and Other category represents miscellaneous corporate expenses that the company counts as negative revenue.	$ -6,707
TOTAL	**$89,950**

artificial intelligence capabilities to Windows 10, Microsoft is opening up the field of artificial intelligence by giving developers access to Microsoft's cloud computing platform, which it calls Azure. The platform provides developers and information technology professionals with software and support services via the internet.

The Microsoft of today, a global leader in its industry, is very different from the small start-up two young men, Bill Gates and Paul Allen, cofounded in 1975. Back then, typewriters, not computers, sat on people's desks. The World Wide Web hadn't been invented yet. There were no smartphones, tablets, or Xboxes. The personal computer revolution was just beginning, and Gates and Allen would be at the forefront of the action.

CHAPTER TWO

MICROSOFT IS BORN

I n 1974, 21-year-old Paul Allen trudged through the streets of Boston, Massachusetts, toward Harvard Square on a cold, snowy day in December. He was on his way to visit his friend, Bill Gates, at Harvard University. Little did Allen know, his life was about to change forever.

As Allen approached Harvard Square, he stopped by a newsstand to browse the magazine rack. The cover of *Popular Electronics* caught his eye. The headline said, "PROJECT BREAKTHROUGH! World's First Minicomputer Kit to Rival Commercial Models . . . ALTAIR 8800." The article inside explained that "the era of the computer in every home—a favorite topic among science fiction writers—has arrived!"[1]

Allen bought the magazine and rushed to Gates's room at Harvard to show him the

A visitor center at the Microsoft headquarters displays an Altair 8800, the early computer that played a role in the company's creation.

article. It was an incredible development. Now, people could buy a kit to assemble a personal computer, and it cost less than $400.[2]

THE ALTAIR 8800

Far away from snowy Boston, in the dry desert of Albuquerque, New Mexico, electronics enthusiast Ed Roberts created the Altair in 1974. Roberts was the head of a company called Micro Instrumentation and Telemetry Systems (MITS).

By today's standards, the Altair was a very primitive version of a personal computer. Users had to assemble the computer themselves, and there was no screen or keyboard. Switches let users give the computer input, and lights flashed the result. The Altair was built around Intel Corporation's 8080 computer chip. The 8080 chip had four times as much memory as the company's previous chip, was three times as powerful, and was relatively easy to write simple programs for. But to make the machine useful, people would have to write those programs.

WRITING BASIC FOR THE ALTAIR

The opportunity for Allen and Gates to put their extensive computer programming skills to work had finally arrived. They decided they would create a program for the Altair that would allow people to use BASIC on the machine. *BASIC* stands for Beginner's All-Purpose Symbolic Instruction Code. BASIC was one of several programming languages in use at the time, and it was the easiest to learn.

Gates contacted Roberts at MITS and told him that they had created a BASIC program for the Altair. He was bluffing. They had not even sat down to write the program yet. Roberts wasn't fooled though. He had many people calling him and saying they had developed software for the Altair. Roberts told Gates what he'd been telling everyone else. The first person to show him a BASIC program that actually worked on the Altair would get a contract with MITS.

For the next eight weeks, Allen and Gates worked feverishly in the Aiken Computer Center at Harvard. What

Gates, *left*, and Allen had a vision for the future of personal computing.

neither of them knew was that the engineers at Intel who had created the 8080 chip had expressed serious doubts about whether it was even possible to create a BASIC program that would be compatible with it. The challenge was especially daunting because Allen and Gates did not have access to an Altair. Roberts had the only Altair in existence in New Mexico. Instead, Gates and Allen read about the Altair's design in the *Popular Electronics* article. They also went to an electronics shop and bought a manual about Intel's 8080 chip.

During the next eight weeks, Allen and Gates worked for days at a time, often with very little sleep. They hired another Harvard student, Monte Davidoff, to help with the project. Finally, the BASIC program was ready. Gates later said that of all the computer code he had written, he was most proud of this BASIC program. "It was the coolest program I ever wrote," he said.[4]

With the BASIC program in hand, Allen flew to Albuquerque to show Roberts how the program worked on the Altair. Because Allen and Gates did not have an Altair themselves, they didn't know whether the program would work when they walked into the room. A very nervous Allen fed the program into the Altair and crossed his fingers. Suddenly, the computer came to life. Allen commanded it to add 2 and 2, and the computer spit out "4." The BASIC program worked. The Altair now had a software language that was easy for people to learn. The personal computer revolution had begun, and Allen and Gates were at the forefront of the movement.

FORMING MICROSOFT

Allen and Gates founded Microsoft on April 4, 1975. They both continued to work on the BASIC program to improve it. On July 22, 1975, Microsoft signed a licensing agreement with MITS. It was a savvy agreement that Gates's father, an experienced lawyer, helped Gates prepare.

The contract gave MITS exclusive rights to use and license the BASIC program, but there was a key provision that would become important in the future. The contract specified that "The Company (MITS) agrees to use its best efforts to license, promote, and commercialize the Program (BASIC). The Company's failure to use its best efforts . . . shall constitute sufficient grounds and reasons to terminate this agreement."[5]

The relationship between Microsoft and MITS was a rocky one, partly because Gates and Roberts didn't get along. They would often get into shouting matches. Gates thought MITS was poorly run. He believed its operation could be made more efficient. Gates was also exasperated by the fact that the Altair's memory boards rarely worked.

"A COMPUTER IN EVERY HOME"

In the early 1970s, corporate leaders at companies such as IBM couldn't imagine why an average person would want a personal computer. But the young Allen and Gates had a very different vision. They both dreamed that someday personal computers would become commonplace. "We wrote our slogan—a very modest slogan—a computer in every home and on every desktop—in 1975," Gates said.[6]

BILL GATES

William Henry Gates III was born in Seattle, Washington, on October 28, 1955. His father, William Henry Gates II, was an attorney, and his mother, Mary, was educated as a schoolteacher. In 1966, Gates memorized the Sermon on the Mount, a complex Bible passage. He recited the passage flawlessly to his church's reverend, Dale Turner. Turner later said, "I needed only to go to his home that day to know that he was something special. I couldn't imagine how an 11-year-old boy could have a mind like that."[7]

In 1967, Gates became a student at Lakeside School, a prestigious private school in Seattle. It was at Lakeside where Gates got his first glimpse of a computer. He was fascinated by the machine. As a teenager, he spent countless hours learning how to program computers. Gates also met his future business partner, Paul Allen, while they were both students at Lakeside.

In 1994, Gates married Melinda French, and the couple went on to have three children. In 1995, at age 39, Gates became the world's richest man with a fortune worth $12.9 billion.[8] Gates served as chief executive officer of Microsoft from 1975 until 2000. Gates then served as Microsoft's chief software architect from 2000 until 2006. In 2005, Queen Elizabeth II bestowed an honorary knighthood on Gates for his contributions to the United Kingdom. In 2008, Gates stepped away entirely from his duties at Microsoft to focus on his charitable work at the Bill & Melinda Gates Foundation. The foundation, one of the largest charitable organizations on the planet, focuses on health care, poverty, and education.

By the 2010s, Gates became known primarily as a philanthropist.

Without the memory boards, the BASIC program could not run.

In 1976, Microsoft landed General Electric and National Cash Register as clients. Revenues for Microsoft's first full year were more than $100,000.[9] In 1977, Gates dropped out of Harvard and joined Allen at Microsoft.

Microsoft's relationship with MITS continued to deteriorate. The contract with MITS prevented Microsoft from selling copies of its BASIC program without MITS's approval. Roberts would not approve sales of the program to his competitors. At first, MITS had no real competitors in the market, but this soon changed as other companies began making computers too. These new computer makers needed software, and Gates saw this need as a huge business opportunity for Microsoft. Even early on, Gates envisioned millions of personal computers across the world all running his company's software.

LEGAL BATTLE WITH MITS

In 1977, Gates and Allen hired lawyers and notified MITS in writing that Microsoft was ending its licensing agreement for the BASIC program, effective in ten days.

The dispute took several months to resolve. During the battle, Roberts sold MITS to a company called Pertec.

Pertec went on to make a huge mistake. Company officials wrote a letter to Microsoft threatening to stop marketing or licensing BASIC. This threat went against the key provision in the original contract between MITS and Microsoft that said Microsoft could end the agreement if MITS failed to promote and license its program. The letter turned out to be a key piece of evidence that allowed Microsoft to win the dispute and end its licensing agreement with Pertec. As a result, Microsoft could freely license and distribute the BASIC software to other companies. This was a huge victory for the young company.

COMPUTER CLUBS FUEL THE COMPUTER REVOLUTION

After the article about the Altair appeared in *Popular Electronics*, people began forming computer clubs across the country. In Northern California, one of the most famous clubs, the Homebrew Computer Club, first met in March 1975 in a garage near Stanford University. More than 30 people showed up for the meeting, one of whom was Steve Wozniak. Wozniak, along with Steve Jobs, would go on to form Apple Computer Company in 1976. Apple would later become a fierce competitor to Microsoft in the personal computer software industry.

CHAPTER THREE

THE IBM DEAL

I n 1980, Microsoft made the deal that industry experts describe as a turning point that made the company what it is today. IBM, an industry leader in making huge mainframe computers, decided to enter the microcomputer market. In that year, Microsoft signed a contract with IBM to provide an operating system for IBM's new line of personal computers. An operating system is a piece of software that helps other software work with the computer's hardware. Microsoft created MS-DOS for IBM. MS-DOS stands for Microsoft Disk Operating System. MS-DOS soared in popularity and became the standard operating system in the computer industry. By 1991, Microsoft was earning more than $200 million a year from MS-DOS sales alone.[1] This success would set the stage for Microsoft to dominate personal computing in the 1990s.

Gates appeared at computer trade shows to promote Microsoft software, including its products for IBM PCs.

A CLASH OF CULTURES

IBM's top-secret decision to begin making microcomputers was codenamed "Project Chess."[2] The company's deal with Microsoft marked the first time IBM had asked an outside vendor to play such a big role in one of its projects. Corporate executives at IBM worried about whether Microsoft could actually deliver what it had promised. IBM and Microsoft were two very different companies.

IBM was a corporate giant. It posted more than $30 billion in annual revenues and had a workforce that was more than half the size of Seattle's population.[3] The company was famous for its extremely conservative culture. It was nicknamed Big Blue because executives came to work in blue suits with white shirts each day. IBM represented the well-established old guard, but some believed the company had become too stuffy and bureaucratic. At IBM, it became difficult to get

MICROSOFT RELOCATES

In 1979, Gates and Allen decided Albuquerque was too far away from the burgeoning technology industry on the West Coast. Both Gates and Allen had grown up in Seattle. They chose to relocate Microsoft to Bellevue, Washington, a suburb of Seattle. In 1986, Microsoft's headquarters moved to nearby Redmond, Washington. Microsoft's Redmond campus was designed to feel like a college campus so it would attract talented young computer programmers.

things done quickly, which is why the company decided to outsource the operating system and software development to Microsoft.

In contrast, Microsoft was a young company, and its culture reflected Gates's competitive personality. Microsoft had only $7 million in annual sales and had fewer than 40 employees, many of whom looked like long-haired hippies.[4] They came to work at the Albuquerque office in shirts and jeans, walked around barefoot, and loved to blare rock music while they coded. Despite the relaxed dress code, Microsoft's employees worked incredibly long hours. Gates, a brilliant programmer in his own right, worked around the clock and demanded the same from his employees. He could be intense and argumentative as he pushed his programmers to make the best products in the industry.

THE ODD COUPLE

Gates was described as intense, highly competitive, argumentative, and prone to throwing tantrums. His partner, Allen, was soft spoken, patient, and much less confrontational. In Microsoft's early years, they divided up their duties to reflect their different strengths. Gates drummed up sales, negotiated deals, and often wrote up the legal contracts himself, even though he was not a lawyer. Allen worked behind the scenes with the programmers and anticipated new developments in the industry. It was Allen's ability to predict where the computer industry was going that helped keep Microsoft one step ahead of its competitors.

When executives from IBM visited Microsoft to meet with Gates, they thought he was an office assistant. Gates was just 24, and he looked younger than that. During the meeting, however, IBM executive Jack Sams said it soon became clear Gates "had the most brilliant mind that I had ever dealt with."[5]

IBM'S PERSONAL COMPUTER

The deal with IBM required Microsoft to develop a computer operating system within a very short period. As luck would have it, Gates and Allen discovered that another company, Seattle Computer Products, had already developed an operating system very similar to what Microsoft needed. Gates bought all rights to the company's operating system, called 86-DOS, for only $50,000.[6] It turned out to be an extremely shrewd business move on Microsoft's part. Microsoft took 86-DOS and turned it into MS-DOS.

IBM's new personal computer debuted to the world on August 12, 1981. Even by industry standards back then, IBM's computer was nothing fancy. It contained a slow Intel chip and had a very limited amount of memory. If a consumer wanted to add on extra features, the price of the computer could rise to more than $5,000. That was a

PAUL ALLEN

Paul Gardner Allen was born on January 21, 1953, in Seattle. His father, Kenneth, was a librarian, and his mother, Edna Faye, was a schoolteacher. When Allen was 12 years old, his parents decided he needed more of an academic challenge and enrolled him at Lakeside School, an exclusive private school in Seattle. During his seventh-grade year, Allen's teacher, Mr. Spock, described Allen as "the most perceptive and thoughtful boy in my class."[7]

Allen met Gates at Lakeside School when he was 14 and Gates was 12. Both boys shared an intense passion for computers and spent countless years as teenagers learning how to program them. After graduating from Lakeside, Allen went to Washington State University in 1972, but he dropped out two years later to take a job at Honeywell in Boston. When Microsoft was founded, Allen was the company's chief technologist. Allen and Gates signed a formal partnership agreement in 1977 that gave Gates 64 percent of Microsoft and Allen 36 percent.[8]

In 1982, Allen was diagnosed with Hodgkin's disease. He left Microsoft in 1983 and eventually recovered successfully from the cancer. When Allen left Microsoft, he retained his stock shares and remained on the company's board of directors until 2000. After leaving Microsoft, Allen founded Vulcan Ventures to manage his business and philanthropic endeavors. Allen loves sports and music. He bought the NBA's Portland Trailblazers in 1988 and the NFL's Seattle Seahawks in 1997. Allen's Experience Music Project, an interactive rock 'n' roll museum that cost $250 million to build, opened in Seattle in June 2000.[9] It was later renamed the Museum of Pop Culture. In 2009, Allen was diagnosed with non-Hodgkin's lymphoma but made another full recovery. In 2018, Allen was listed as number 44 on the Forbes Billionaire list with a fortune worth $21.7 billion. Allen has given more than $2 billion to charity.[10]

Allen is also interested in naval history and owns a research vessel that has discovered several sunken ships.

big price tag, especially compared with the Apple II and other computers on the market that sold for less than $2,000.[11]

In addition to MS-DOS, Microsoft developed software for the computer that included a BASIC-writing program and a game called *Adventure*. IBM's personal computers became a big hit. As Lincoln Spector wrote in an article for *PC World*, "It isn't the first personal computer by a long shot. But the IBM PC is the first from a company that's respected by corporate America."[12] Computer sales skyrocketed. IBM's computers soon became more popular than those of its competitors, including the Apple II. IBM had expected to sell approximately 250,000 personal computers during the next five years.[13] By the end of 1983, it had sold more than 500,000 of them.[14]

CLONES HIT THE MARKET

IBM's success caught the attention of other computer hardware companies. When IBM built its personal computer, the company adopted an open architecture. This meant the computer was built using components and technology that already existed in the marketplace. IBM didn't own the design of its personal computer. Soon, other computer companies began to piggyback on IBM's

The original IBM PC was bulky and slow by today's standards, but it became popular quickly in the early 1980s.

success by manufacturing clones, or copies, of IBM's popular computer.

Companies such as AT&T, Sperry, Texas Instruments, and National Cash Register entered the clone market. As a result, the number of personal computers available to consumers rose, driving the personal computer's price down. The rise of the clone market hurt IBM's computer sales but greatly benefited Microsoft. Because Microsoft owned the rights to MS-DOS, it could sell MS-DOS to companies making the clones.

When IBM and Microsoft signed the original deal, neither company had anticipated the rise of the clone market. IBM executives thought they had gotten a good deal because they paid Microsoft only $286,000 for development of MS-DOS.[15] IBM executives made it very clear at the outset of the deal that Microsoft would retain all rights to sell the software it developed for IBM's personal computers. At the time, IBM was focused on building personal computers that could outsell Apple. IBM executives wanted nothing to do with developing the software, which was why they sought out Microsoft in the first place.

As other computer companies began copying IBM's personal computers, MS-DOS became more valuable than the computers themselves. It was easy enough for other computer hardware companies to build replicas of IBM's personal computer. IBM employee Mark Dean said, "Anyone who could find a garage and procure a few parts could build one."[17] What the hardware companies really needed, however, was the operating system that made the computers run. Selling MS-DOS to the hardware companies provided a large and steady stream of revenue for Microsoft, setting the stage for Microsoft to grow into the global leader it is today.

CHAPTER FOUR

THE BIRTH OF WINDOWS

Following the success of MS-DOS, Gates turned his attention to Microsoft's next big project: developing Windows, a new operating system for personal computers. The driving force behind developing Windows came from Gates's desire to make computers easier for people to use. With MS-DOS, users had to type in commands on their keyboards to tell computers what to do. But researchers in Palo Alto, California, had discovered an easier and faster way for people to use computers. It was based on a small pointing device that Douglas Engelbart invented in 1963: the mouse.

GRAPHICAL USER INTERFACE

In the early 1970s, Engelbart's invention caught the attention of researchers at Xerox Corporation's Palo Alto Research Center (PARC).

Like other software at the time, Windows came on 5.25-inch (13.3 cm) floppy disks.

Researchers at PARC went on to develop the graphical user interface. A graphical user interface allowed users to operate their computers more intuitively, using a mouse to point and click on images on the computer screen. With the graphical user interface, users would no longer have to type in commands on their keyboards to operate their computers.

It was Allen's responsibility at Microsoft to keep on top of new research developments in the computer industry. Charles Simonyi, a lead programmer at PARC who later left to work for Microsoft, gave Allen a demonstration of how the graphical user interface worked. Allen immediately thought, "Wow! This is going to change everything."[1] When Allen used the computer mouse for the first time, it felt like a natural extension of his arm. Pointing and clicking with the mouse was much faster than typing in keyboard commands, Allen realized.

XEROX'S MISSED OPPORTUNITIES

The graphical user interface technology that computer users around the world take for granted today was developed by Xerox Corporation's PARC. In his memoir, *Idea Man*, Paul Allen said PARC anticipated nearly every major computer trend in the industry. Unfortunately, PARC's parent company, Xerox, never realized the significance of the new technologies its researchers developed and failed to get the ideas to the marketplace. As a result, Xerox missed out on opportunities to influence the personal computer market.

DEVELOPING WINDOWS

Other companies heard about the graphical user interface too and were rushing to get personal computers with this new technology on the market. In 1983, Apple introduced Lisa, the first personal computer with a graphical user interface and a mouse. Lisa also carried a steep price tag, costing approximately $10,000.[2]

In November 1983, Gates announced to the press that Microsoft would soon be releasing its own operating system with a graphical user interface, Windows. In fact, Microsoft had not designed Windows yet. Little did Gates realize that it would take two years before the first version of Windows was finally released in 1985. Along the way, the development of Windows was beset by both technical and managerial problems.

Developing Windows was a huge technical challenge for Microsoft's programmers. The Windows system would require a lot of memory to run on a personal computer. The problem was that most IBM-compatible computers at the time didn't have enough memory to do this. The major challenge for the programmers was to write code for Windows to run efficiently. It was a complex project that involved a lot of record-keeping, testing, and retesting.

Many programmers felt Gates micromanaged the Windows project. He closely oversaw the development of Windows on a day-to-day basis. He kept changing his mind about how the graphics on Windows should look and often added new features. Making a lot of changes cost the company time and therefore money. Microsoft's programmers began to fall behind, and the release of Windows was pushed back several times between 1983 and 1985. Gates frequently argued with and berated Microsoft's programmers, which caused employee morale to nose-dive.

WINDOWS IN THE EARLY YEARS

In November 1985, Microsoft finally released its first version of Windows. The first version wasn't really a new

The new Windows operating system had advanced features, but it failed to catch on upon its initial release.

operating system itself. Instead, it was an application that ran on top of MS-DOS. The first version of Windows ran only on MS-DOS computers that were compatible with IBM's personal computers. Windows was designed for people to use a mouse to point and click on images on the screen. Back then, however, few IBM users owned a mouse.

The first version of Windows was a flop. The personal computers of the time did not have enough memory and speed to take advantage of Windows's best features. Due to numerous delays in developing Windows, software developers were unable to create programs for the finished product in time for its release. This meant there were few other software programs available that could run on the system.

It wasn't until the third version of Windows came out in 1990 that a large amount of software became available. Windows 3.0 still used MS-DOS as its underlying system to run programs. Gates clung to his vision that Windows would make IBM-compatible computers as easy to use as Apple's popular Macintosh computer, which used a mouse and had come out in 1984.

Gates's hopes paid off. Within four months of its release, Windows 3.0 sold one million copies.[4] Consumers could purchase an IBM-compatible personal computer for $2,500, equal to approximately $5,000 in 2018. They could add a copy of Windows 3.0 for $150. This setup was much less expensive than the $4,000 Macintosh.[5] In 1990, Microsoft became the first computer software company to earn $1 billion in revenue.[6]

WINDOWS THROUGH THE YEARS

Microsoft has released several versions of Windows since its initial release in 1985. Windows 95, released in 1995, introduced the "Start" menu, a part of the screen users could click to access their most-used programs. Microsoft's first web browser, Internet Explorer, was also introduced in updated versions of Windows 95. Windows 2000, released in early 2000, was based on Windows NT, another version of Windows intended for corporate use, which no longer used MS-DOS as its underlying technology.

Windows 95 became a global smash hit after its release.

In 2001, Microsoft released Windows XP. Considered one of the best versions of Windows, it was Microsoft's longest-running operating system until it was replaced by Windows Vista in 2007. Windows Vista was not popular with consumers. It was plagued with bugs and ran slowly on older computers, even those that had been declared compatible with it. In 2009, Windows 7 replaced Vista. It was intended to fix all the problems users experienced with Vista.

In 2012, Microsoft radically changed the Windows interface in Windows 8. Instead of a Start button and Start menu, which were designed for use with a mouse, Windows 8 had large icons better suited for use with a touch screen. This change was not welcomed by many desktop computer users, who preferred to use a mouse and keyboard instead of a touch screen. The Windows Store, which offers a way for users to buy and download applications, was also introduced.

CHANGING THE WORLD

In a 2015 article for *eWeek*, Wayne Rash estimated that more than 90 percent of all computers in the world ran Windows.[7] Over time, Windows has proven to be easy to learn and reliable enough to earn a place in people's daily lives. "Microsoft arguably touches more lives on a daily basis than any other corporation on Earth," said Paul Allen in his 2011 memoir. "More than a billion copies of Windows are in use around the world."[8]

WINDOWS 10 TODAY

Microsoft's Windows 10, released in 2015, evolved directly from Windows NT. The operating system runs on many devices, including desktop computers, smartphones, and tablets. Windows 10 includes Cortana, Microsoft's virtual personal office assistant. Cortana responds to voice commands, so users can ask Cortana questions. Users can set calendar appointments, ask about the weather, play music, and take notes. Users can also type in questions and commands for Cortana. Cortana uses Microsoft's Bing search engine. When a user asks Cortana something it doesn't know, the program automatically searches for the answer using the built-in Bing search engine.

Windows 10 also includes Microsoft's new web browser, Edge. It is designed to run more efficiently than Internet Explorer, although the latest version of Internet Explorer is still available in Windows 10 too.

THE POPULARITY OF MICROSOFT OFFICE

In 1983, Microsoft released a word processing application called Microsoft Word. It was developed for the IBM personal computer and its clones. The program included

Microsoft's Office programs are now available on many different platforms, including smartphones.

a variety of fonts, and it worked with the latest printer technology. Microsoft Word received only mediocre reviews because some users believed it was too technical and difficult to learn.

Microsoft's Excel spreadsheet program received much better reviews when it came out in 1985. Unlike the Word program, Excel was designed to work on Apple's Macintosh rather than the IBM personal computer and its clones. In addition to Word and Excel, Microsoft purchased an application originally called Presenter from Forethought, Inc., for $14 million.[9] Microsoft renamed the application PowerPoint. With PowerPoint, users can develop slide presentations with graphics.

In 1989, Microsoft bundled its most popular applications, including Word, Excel, and PowerPoint, into a single package called Microsoft Office. Businesses liked buying applications from one software company. Through the years, Microsoft released many versions of Office that included new features. In 1995, a Mail program was included in Microsoft Office 3.0. Eventually, the Mail application was replaced by Microsoft's Outlook. In response to the growing popularity of Google's productivity suite, known then as Google Apps, Microsoft introduced the Office 365 service. With Office 365, consumers can purchase subscriptions to access Microsoft Office applications online through a web browser. Documents are stored online, so they can be accessed anywhere rather than being tied to a specific computer. Microsoft Office is the world's most popular productivity suite. It is estimated to be running on more than one billion devices worldwide.[10]

MICROSOFT GOES PUBLIC

On March 13, 1986, Microsoft went public. This means that it made stock available on the New York Stock Exchange. When a person buys stock, they are making an investment. If the company does well, the stock price goes up. Stockholders earn money. Microsoft stock initially sold for $25.75 per share. Within weeks, the price rose to $35.50 per share. In March 1987, the stock reached $90.75 per share.[11] Gates and Allen, both owners of significant Microsoft stock, became billionaires. As Paul Allen wrote in his memoir, *Idea Man*, "I sold 200,000 shares and kept the rest. . . . Overnight I was $175 million richer. . . . By 1990, at age 37, I'd become a billionaire. By 1996, I'd be one ten times over."[12]

CHAPTER FIVE

THE INTERNET REVOLUTION

I n the 1990s, Microsoft was the undisputed leader in the computer industry, and the company was still growing rapidly. But Gates wasn't basking in his company's success. Instead, he remained as competitive and driven as ever. In 1995, in an interview with journalist Tom Brokaw, Gates said technology was "a very scary business. If you fall behind technically, no matter how much your past success has been, it's no guarantee that you'll keep doing well in the future."[1]

THE INTERNET TIDAL WAVE

In 1995, Bill Gates wrote an internal memo to Microsoft employees called "The Internet Tidal Wave." In the memo, he declared the internet to be "the most important single development to come along since the IBM PC was introduced in

Gates was determined to take advantage of the internet's potential, but Microsoft's online efforts also attracted the attention of government regulators.

1981." Gates said the internet was crucial to every part of Microsoft's business and assigned the internet as the company's highest priority. "I want every product plan to try and go overboard on Internet features," he wrote.[2]

Gates encouraged his employees to use the internet. He said the amount of information available on the internet was amazing. He likened it to a positive feedback loop. Users published content on the internet. This content attracted more users, who then published more content, and so on. According to Gates, it was easier to find information on the web than it was on Microsoft's internal networks. "This inversion where a public network solves a problem better than a private network is quite stunning," he wrote.[3]

THE "SILICON BULLY"

In the early 1990s, *Business Month* magazine wrote an article about Bill Gates titled "The Silicon Bully: How Long Can Bill Gates Kick Sand in the Face of the Computer Industry?"[4] Microsoft's unparalleled success in the computer software industry had caused deep resentment toward the company and Gates himself. Many of Microsoft's competitors accused Gates of breaking the rules and not playing fairly. Although many of Microsoft's detractors refused to give their names when quoted in the media, Gates's competitors claimed Microsoft had a pattern of stealing rivals' ideas, especially the ideas of smaller, less powerful companies, and using them in its own products.

Gates predicted that soon almost every personal computer would be connected to the internet. He thought the market for personal computers would remain strong because consumers would buy personal computers to have access to the internet.

Gates discussed Microsoft's competitors in the computer software industry, including Novell, Sun Microsystems, Apple, and Netscape. He called Netscape "a new competitor 'born' on the Internet."[5] In 1994, Netscape had launched its web browser, Navigator 1.0. At the time, there was no real competition in the browser market. By early 1995, Netscape's browser had captured 70 percent of the market share.[6] Gates made it clear that Microsoft needed to match and beat Netscape's offerings.

He also told his employees to study the way Microsoft's competitors used websites to introduce consumers to their products. Gates said it was important for Microsoft's home page to contain relevant and compelling content about the company. The internet would allow Microsoft to bypass the press and communicate directly with consumers. The press would not have an opportunity to miscommunicate information to the public. "Customers will come to our 'home page' in

Netscape Navigator won an early lead in the browser market.

unbelievable numbers and find out everything we want them to know," he wrote.[7]

Gates called the internet both an incredible opportunity for Microsoft and an incredible challenge. The internet was changing rapidly, and Microsoft's products would need to change quickly too, he said. Gates believed Microsoft's greatest strengths going forward were the company's people and the public's broad acceptance of Windows and Office.

THE BROWSER WARS

In August 1995, Microsoft released Windows 95, but the operating system didn't include a built-in web browser. Microsoft licensed code from Spyglass, a smaller company, to develop its first browser, Internet Explorer. Microsoft then released a separate add-on pack called Microsoft Plus!, which included Internet Explorer. Microsoft also began working on build ng Explorer directly into Windows itself, so it would become Windows's default browser. By bundling Internet Explorer with its Windows operating system, Microsoft took advantage of Windows's popularity to get users to switch from Navigator to its own Explorer browser.

Early versions of Internet Explorer were plagued with security issues, and industry experts warned users to avoid Explorer and choose an alternative browser. Despite its flaws, however, Explorer became very popular with consumers. In 1998, Internet Explorer surpassed Netscape's Navigator to become the most popular browser on the market. At one point in 2003, Internet Explorer captured approximately 95 percent of the global browser market.[8]

In the 2000s, Internet Explorer began to face competition from new browsers such as Mozilla's Firefox and Apple's Safari. Google also released its Chrome browser. Soon, Explorer lost its place as the most popular web browser. With its launch of Windows 10 and its new Edge browser, Microsoft gradually began phasing out Internet Explorer.

HEADED TO COURT

In July 1994, Microsoft signed an agreement with the US Department of Justice (DOJ) that forbade Microsoft from using its Windows operating system dominance to crush its competition. In October 1997, the DOJ filed a complaint against Microsoft claiming that the company violated the agreement when it demanded personal computer manufacturers include Internet Explorer with the computers they sold before being able to install Windows 95 on those computers. The DOJ demanded that Microsoft pay a multimillion-dollar fine.

On May 18, 1998, the DOJ and 20 state attorneys general filed an antitrust lawsuit against Microsoft. In *United States v. Microsoft*, the government alleged that Microsoft abused its market dominance when it bundled Internet Explorer with its Windows operating system to beat out competition from Netscape's web browser. The DOJ claimed that Microsoft was violating the Sherman Antitrust Act. This law, passed in 1890, prohibits activities that restrict competition in the marketplace. The idea behind the law is that when businesses compete for customers to buy their products, they produce the most innovative products at lower prices. Without competition in the marketplace, a business has no incentive to produce a better product and can charge consumers higher prices. The Sherman Antitrust Act was enacted to preserve competition between businesses in the marketplace.

During the court case, the press painted Gates

SPECIAL ANTITRUST CONCERNS IN THE TECHNOLOGY INDUSTRY

In December 1997, the *Economist* ran an article explaining why there were special concerns about businesses violating antitrust laws in the technology sector. The first idea is that the technology industry has "ever-increasing returns." This means that when a company wins a technological race, that company has an advantage in the next race. For example, Microsoft won the race to develop the most widely used operating system in the world, Windows, and this gave the company an advantage when it entered the browser wars. The second idea is known as "network externalities."[9] This theory says that when a product is highly used, it deters competitors from entering that market. For example, Windows is the dominating operating system. Customers would be highly unlikely to switch to a different operating system because switching would require a lot of time and effort. Other businesses, therefore, are discouraged from developing new operating systems and selling them to consumers.

as a bully who used extremely aggressive and unfair business practices to crush Microsoft's competition. Gates didn't help his image when he testified in videotaped depositions and appeared arrogant, defensive, and confrontational. In the public, there was broad anti-Gates and anti-Microsoft sentiment.

Gates appeared via a video feed at a news conference with his lawyers during the antitrust trial.

On April 3, 2000, a judge ruled that Microsoft had violated antitrust laws and consistently acted to hold on to its power over industry competitors. Microsoft had unlawfully attached Internet Explorer to Windows. Two months later, the judge ordered Microsoft to be divided into two companies, one for operating systems and the other for software. In 2001, a federal appeals court reversed the order to break up Microsoft. The parties in the case agreed to a settlement, which another judge approved in 2002.

Even though Microsoft remained intact, the case took a huge toll on the company, in large part because it had badly distracted Gates from Microsoft's day-to-day operations. In January 2000, Gates announced he was stepping down as Microsoft's chief executive officer (CEO) and would become the company's chief software architect instead. Gates was

THE EUROPEAN UNION WEIGHS IN

In 2002, the European Union (EU) began its own separate probe into Microsoft. Officials there determined that the company was abusing its monopoly in the operating system industry. In 2009, the EU forced Microsoft to offer customers the ability to easily download an alternative browser rather than locking customers into using Internet Explorer.

still Microsoft's undisputed technical leader. Steve Ballmer replaced Gates as Microsoft's new CEO.

SEARCH ENGINE COMPETITION

In 1998, in an interview with *New Yorker* writer Ken Auletta, Gates said he didn't fear Microsoft's established competitors such as Sun Microsystems, Oracle, or Netscape. What he did fear was "someone in a garage who is devising something completely new."[10] Microsoft's own history proved just how powerful a start-up company run by intelligent, young entrepreneurs could become in the computer industry.

That's how Google arrived on the scene. As content on the internet exploded, users needed a better way to search through all that information. While Microsoft was embroiled in the government's antitrust lawsuit, Larry Page and Sergey Brin, both in their mid-twenties, created a powerful new internet search engine. They formed a small start-up company called Google in California in 1998.

Although there were many search engines in the 1990s, including Yahoo!, Google's search engine was the first to rank results intelligently, placing more popular

Sergey Brin, *left*, and Larry Page built Google into the dominant search engine, far outpacing Microsoft's efforts to enter the market.

pages first. Page and Brin focused on making Google's search engine fast. Both the home page and the results page had to load quickly. Google didn't use Microsoft's Windows as an operating system on the computers that ran its search services. Instead, Page and Brin built their own system that ran on a customized version of the free Linux operating system.

By 2001, Google had become the most popular stand-alone search engine on the web. Page and Brin feared that Microsoft would enter the search engine market and try to crush Google as it had done with Netscape. Although Microsoft had launched Microsoft Network (MSN) in 1995, people didn't think of MSN as a search engine in the same way that they did Google. MSN was originally created as an online service that provided access to the internet and specialized content for a subscription fee. In 2006, Microsoft launched Live Search, but this search engine trailed behind Yahoo! and Google.

In 2009, Microsoft released its new search engine, Bing. Microsoft called Bing

MICROSOFT PARTNERS WITH YAHOO! AND FACEBOOK

In 2009, Microsoft entered a partnership with Yahoo! in which Yahoo!'s search engine would be powered by Bing. The following year, Facebook agreed to show Bing results to users who were searching the web from within Facebook. At the time, Facebook had more than 400 million users and was the second-most-visited site behind Google.[11] Facebook removed the Bing search feature from its service in 2014, though the company continued to partner with Microsoft in other areas.

a "decision engine," meaning that it displayed more information in results pages so that it could help users choose the best results.[12] Bing targets four major search categories: shopping, local, travel, and health. Despite Microsoft's introduction of Bing, Google remains the most popular search engine in the United States. In January 2018, Google generated 63.2 percent of all search queries in the United States versus Microsoft's 23.7 percent share.[13]

CHAPTER SIX

MICROSOFT ENTERS GAMING

When Gates and Allen cofounded Microsoft in 1975, they dreamed of a computer in every home and on every desktop. More than two decades later Gates was thinking about a computer in every living room. This time, however, the computer would be a video game console. At the time, Sony's PlayStation was very popular. Gates worried that Sony's console might evolve into an entertainment and media device that would eventually replace the personal computer. Gates decided Microsoft needed to enter the gaming market.

THE XBOX

In March 2000, Gates gave a glimpse of Microsoft's new gaming console, the Xbox, at the Game Developers Conference. The underlying

Gates unveiled the Xbox's final design to the public in January 2001.

Microsoft invested heavily in marketing its entrance into the competitive video game industry.

technologies behind the Xbox were similar to those used in PCs. This made it relatively easy for traditional software developers to create games for the Xbox. The Xbox also had twice as much processing power as the popular Sony PlayStation 2, which was slated for release in the United States that fall. Critics, however, were skeptical that the Xbox was anything more than a fancy personal computer. They doubted that a company known for operating systems and productivity software could succeed against experienced video game companies.

In November 2001, Gates was on hand for Xbox's launch at a toy store in Times Square in New York City. The Xbox cost $299, and its competition included the similarly priced PlayStation 2 and Nintendo's GameCube, which was $100 cheaper. More than one million Xboxes were sold within three weeks of the console's release.[1] Many games were available on all three platforms, but some titles were exclusive to a single console. The Halo franchise of first-person shooters became Xbox's signature exclusive series.

THE XBOX GOES LIVE

One year after the Xbox came out, Microsoft launched Xbox Live, a gaming network that allowed users to play online with other people from around the world. More than 150,000 people subscribed to Xbox Live within its first week of release.[2] By 2018, Xbox Live had more than 50 million members.[3]

With Xbox Live, Microsoft set the standard for online gaming. The service's main features included a Friends

THE SUCCESS OF *HALO*

In 2000, Microsoft purchased the game *Halo* from Bungie Studios for $30 million. The creators at Bungie turned *Halo* into a first-person shooter game that was exclusive to the Xbox. Microsoft's purchase of *Halo* turned out to be a smart move, as the game was a huge success and drove sales of the Xbox. More than one million copies of *Halo* were sold within the first few months of the game's release. When *Halo 2* came out, more than 2.5 million Xboxes were sold within the first 24 hours of the game's release. *Halo 2* itself earned $125 million in sales, making it the most successful launch of any entertainment product in history at that time.[4] Microsoft eventually founded a new game studio, 343 Industries, that would be solely dedicated to developing new Halo games.

List, voice chat, and a Gamertag, a single identifying name that a user could use for any games played on the Xbox. Microsoft could use Xbox Live to provide updates and new features for its consoles. Users could easily download extra maps, levels, and modes for existing games. Xbox Live became an integral part of the Xbox and its successors. It created a multiplayer experience for gamers and built an online gaming community.

WHY DID THE XBOX FAIL IN JAPAN?

Microsoft worked hard to gain a foothold in the Japanese market, but it didn't work. Japanese game developers felt the Xbox was designed for American gamers and featured games that Japanese gamers wouldn't be interested in. The Japanese developers were also reluctant to support Microsoft and alienate local companies such as Sony. In addition, the design of the Xbox itself reinforced the notion that it was a Western gaming console. The Japanese thought the Xbox was too large and cumbersome. It was made out of inexpensive black plastic, and the original game controller was notoriously large and bulky. Many Japanese gamers preferred a more lightweight, sleeker design.

THE XBOX 360

Four years after Microsoft launched its original Xbox, it released a successor, the Xbox 360. Microsoft timed the 2005 release of the Xbox 360 ahead of its competitors, Sony's PlayStation 3 and Nintendo's Wii. Sales of the new console soared in North America and Europe but lagged behind in Japan. By the end of 2005, Microsoft had sold more than

1.5 million units of the Xbox 360. By 2010, this number had grown to 39 million consoles in households around the world.[5]

In 2009 and 2010, Microsoft made significant improvements to the Xbox 360. The first was the launch of a motion and voice control sensor called the Kinect that users could plug into the console. Rather than simply sitting on the couch, players could get up, move around, and speak to control their games. The second was a redesign of the console that included a slimmer body, additional USB ports, and built-in wireless internet support. This new version, the Xbox 360 S, came out in 2010.

Sales of the Xbox 360 remained strong. In December 2012, Microsoft announced that it had sold 75 million consoles. Although this figure trailed behind Nintendo's Wii, it surpassed sales of Sony's PlayStation 3 by approximately five million consoles.[6]

GOODBYE ORIGINAL XBOX

The release of the Xbox 360 signaled the end of Microsoft's production of and support for the original Xbox. In retrospect, the original Xbox did not live up to Microsoft's lofty expectations. Microsoft originally predicted there would be 50 million Xboxes in households around the world. The actual number turned out to be 24 million consoles. Although the Xbox outsold Nintendo's GameCube, its sales came nowhere close to matching those of Sony's PlayStation 2, which sold more than 153 million consoles.[7]

THE NEXT GENERATION

In 2013, Microsoft launched its third gaming console, the Xbox One. The company touted the Xbox One as an all-in-one entertainment center that offered games, TV, movies, music, and video calls. The console also included a new version of the Kinect device, which Microsoft said would be better at analyzing users' body movements. In 2016, Microsoft introduced a smaller version of the Xbox One called the Xbox One S. It was 40 percent smaller than the original Xbox One console, and both the console and controller were white instead of black.[8]

THE "RED RING OF DEATH" ERROR

The early models of the Xbox 360 were plagued with hardware and software problems, including the ominous error nicknamed the Red Ring of Death. The problem, linked to overheating components, occurred when the Xbox 360 crashed and a red ring lit up around the console's power button. Microsoft had to repair and replace the consoles, which cost the company an estimated $1 billion.[10]

Microsoft's rival, Sony, also launched a new version of its console, the PlayStation 4, in 2013. By 2017, it was clear that Sony was dominating this generation of the console market, with the PlayStation 4 selling twice as many consoles worldwide as the Xbox One.[9] Despite lagging behind Sony, Microsoft launched another new console, the Xbox One X, in November 2017. The X was compatible with all Xbox One games, but it also had significant additional computing power that newer games could take advantage of. Its price tag was higher than those of its predecessors too. Costing $499 at launch, the Xbox One X was almost twice as expensive as the Xbox One.[11]

Microsoft began phasing out Kinect support in its later revisions of the Xbox One. Users can hook up a Kinect sensor with a USB adaptor, but there is no dedicated port for it on the Xbox One X. Instead, gamers can use Microsoft's personal assistant, Cortana, on the Xbox One X to get voice control functionality. A user can say "Hey Cortana" into the headset's microphone to bring up a Cortana window. Cortana responds to voice commands, and it can launch games, browse Xbox menus, and give weather information and sports scores.

MICROSOFT BUYS MINECRAFT

Minecraft is one of the most popular video games ever created. Since its launch in 2009, *Minecraft* has been downloaded 100 million times.[12] The game was developed by Markus Persson, who founded the Swedish game studio Mojang. In 2014, Microsoft purchased the *Minecraft* game and Mojang for $2.5 billion.[13] At the time of purchase, Microsoft said it was committed to keeping *Minecraft* available across all game platforms, including those owned by its competitors.

CHAPTER SEVEN

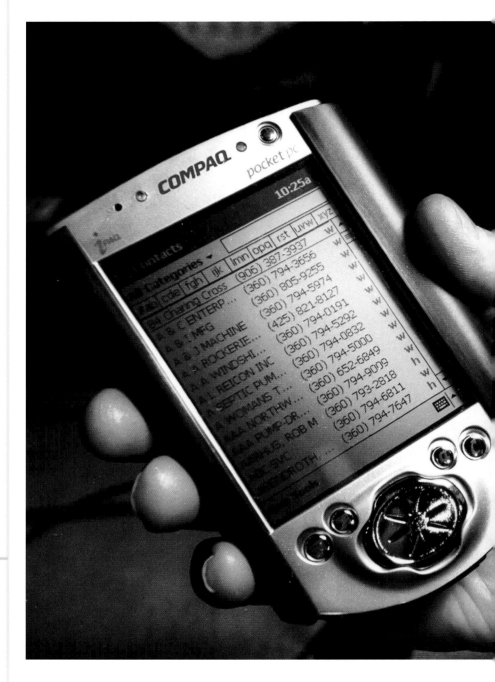

GOING MOBILE

n the 1950s and 1960s, computers were giant machines that took up entire rooms. Then the personal computer arrived. Computers became much smaller machines that could fit easily on desktops. Today, computers fit in the palms of people's hands as smartphones. Although Microsoft played a dominant role in the personal computer revolution, the company did not have the same success when it tried to break into the smartphone market.

THE EARLY SMARTPHONES AND WINDOWS MOBILE

IBM is credited with developing the first smartphone. In 1994, IBM's Simon Personal Communicator went on sale to the public. It was a telephone that could send and receive emails and faxes. Its operating system was a modified version of MS-DOS. It sold 50,000 units, but IBM kept it on the market for only six months.[1]

Devices running Microsoft's Pocket PC operating system were the precursors to the sleek, powerful smartphones of today.

THE POWER OF SMARTPHONES

In his 2012 book *Digital Wars*, technology journalist Charles Arthur described the dramatic way in which smartphones affected people's everyday lives. He wrote, "Smartphones bring the internet to places it might never have reached before; they are handheld computers that are also . . . connected to the internet. In sub-Saharan Africa there are 14 mobile phones for every PC; as smartphones become cheaper that ratio will grow. . . . And, while even a laptop PC battery will run out in less than a day, a smartphone will last at least that long, and needs less energy to recharge."[2]

In 1996, Nokia debuted the Nokia 9000 Communicator. It was a telephone with a full keyboard, and it was the first such device to include a web browser. It could send emails and faxes and also had word processing and spreadsheet capabilities. The term *smartphone* was coined in 1999 when Ericsson launched its Ericsson R380. Also in 1999, the company Research in Motion launched the BlackBerry 850. This smartphone focused on email and had a large keyboard. The line of BlackBerry devices became very popular with business users.

In the early years of smartphones, Microsoft focused on developing a version of its popular Windows operating system for mobile devices. In 2000, Microsoft released its Pocket PC operating system. It was designed to look like a smaller version of Windows 98. The company renamed the operating system Windows Mobile in 2003. A handful of companies, including Hewlett-Packard, Motorola, HTC, and Samsung, manufactured smartphones with the Windows Mobile operating system.

These early smartphones were designed for business people. The average consumer was focused on general cell phone use and wasn't interested in purchasing smartphones. The early smartphones were not seen as devices that ordinary people would use on a daily basis. This perception changed dramatically when Apple launched the iPhone in 2007.

THE SMARTPHONE REVOLUTION

When Apple CEO Steve Jobs introduced the iPhone, he described it as "a revolutionary and magical product that is literally five years ahead of any other mobile phone."[3] Jobs was right. Smartphones soared in popularity with consumers after Apple introduced the iPhone. Over a ten-year period, iPhone sales grew from 270,000

GATES AND JOBS'S RELATIONSHIP

Gates and Jobs were long-standing business rivals. In 1995, Jobs admitted that Apple had lost to Microsoft in the personal computer industry. "The desktop computer industry is dead," Jobs said. "Innovation has virtually ceased. Microsoft dominates with very little innovation. That's over. Apple lost."[4] Although Apple failed to overtake Microsoft in the personal computer arena, Jobs didn't quit. Apple went on to triumph over Microsoft in the smartphone market.

The original iPhone changed the consumer electronics landscape forever.

units in the third quarter of 2007 to 78.3 million units in the first quarter of 2017.[5] According to data from the Pew Research Center, a polling company, almost two-thirds of US citizens owned a smartphone by April 2015.[6]

Unlike the smartphones before it, the iPhone was designed for everyday users. It was the first smartphone to have a touch screen surface that was reliable and easy to use with a user's fingers. Before the iPhone, people often used a penlike pointing device called a stylus on touch screens. The iPhone also had a very simple design that appealed to consumers. It had only one button on its face, the "home" button, and three buttons around its edges: two volume buttons and the power button. The iPhone used Apple's operating system, which would later be called iOS. With iOS, users could enjoy browsing the internet as they would on a desktop computer. They could listen to music, watch videos, send and receive emails, and make phone calls. In 2008, Apple introduced the App Store. Now, software developers could make new applications for the iPhone, and users could purchase and install them. Soon, there were tens of thousands of applications available.

In 2008, Google also entered the smartphone market with its new operating system, called Android. Google offered its Android system for free, so any device manufacturer could design and sell its own phones running Android. The operating system used Google services for web searches, email, and video.

By 2009, there were seven major mobile operating systems. Windows Mobile was quickly losing ground to the iPhone, which ran Apple's iOS operating system, and Android. One report showed Windows Mobile dropping from 13.9 percent of the global smartphone market in 2002 to 9 percent in 2009. By 2012, Apple's iOS and Google's Android dominated the market.[7]

Although consumers wanted Windows on their personal computers, they didn't seem to need Windows on their smartphones. As Brian Chen wrote in *Wired* magazine in 2009, "Microsoft Windows continues to dominate the PC market with a 90 percent market-share

Windows Mobile failed to make a dent in the mobile operating system market, so Microsoft searched for new ways to compete against Apple and Google.

stronghold, but when it comes to smartphones, Microsoft is getting beat up worse than a mustachioed villain in a Jackie Chan movie."[8]

Some industry experts felt Windows Mobile wasn't more popular with consumers because it didn't have a strong selection of apps to go with it. In addition, people felt the Windows Mobile system was heavily focused on business users and had failed to include features that would appeal to the average consumer.

WINDOWS PHONE

To compete more effectively against Apple and Google, Microsoft shifted its focus away from Windows Mobile to its new operating system, Windows Phone. In 2010, the first smartphones with the Windows Phone operating system became available to the public, but sales were low. By the end of 2011, Android had captured more than 50 percent of the smartphone market.[9] Microsoft searched for a way to catch up.

In 2011, Microsoft entered into a partnership with the mobile phone company Nokia. Windows Phone became the new operating system for Nokia's smartphones.

Nokia executive Stephen Elop introduced new devices running Windows Phone in 2014.

Nokia's Lumia 800 and Lumia 710 were among the first smartphones to run the Windows Phone software.

In 2014, Microsoft bought Nokia's devices and services division for approximately $7.2 billion.[10] After the deal, the division became a subsidiary of Microsoft and was renamed Microsoft Mobile. Ballmer championed the deal because he wanted Microsoft to become a "devices and services" company.[11] By acquiring Nokia, Microsoft entered into the phone hardware business.

The purchase of Nokia turned out to be a big mistake for Microsoft. In 2015, 96.8 percent of all smartphones sold were either iPhones or Android phones. Microsoft had captured only 2.5 percent of the smartphone market.[12] Windows Phone was renamed Windows 10 Mobile. In 2016, Microsoft dismantled Microsoft Mobile and laid off thousands of former Nokia employees. In 2017, Microsoft's Joe Belfiore announced that Microsoft was no longer developing new features or hardware for Windows 10 Mobile.

Industry experts cited Microsoft's failure to attract developers to create third-party apps for the Windows Phone operating system as one of the biggest reasons Microsoft lost out to Apple and Google. Some companies that initially created apps for the operating system simply stopped updating them due to a lack of users. American Airlines, Chase Bank, Bank of America, NBC, and Pinterest all discontinued their Windows Phone apps.

Though Microsoft had departed the phone hardware business, it continued to produce software for other smartphone platforms. Versions of Office are available for iOS and Android. For portable hardware, the company shifted away from smartphones and put more resources into its tablet and laptop efforts.

CHAPTER **EIGHT**

MICROSOFT SURFACE

When Gates and Allen cofounded Microsoft in 1975, they focused on developing software products that set the industry standard and dominated the market. This turned out to be a wise and very profitable direction for Microsoft. The company made its name in software.

In 2012, however, Ballmer introduced the Surface tablet. It was the first time in the company's history that Microsoft had made a personal computer. Microsoft entered the hardware market with high expectations for the Surface tablet, but it wasn't until the third generation of this device that it began to catch on with consumers and business users.

When it introduced its line of Surface tablets, Microsoft was making its largest-ever investment in the hardware industry.

THE ORIGINAL MICROSOFT SURFACE

The name "Microsoft Surface" first came into play when Microsoft built a 30-inch (76 cm) flat computer tablet into a coffee table in 2008. The idea to build computers into flat surfaces such as coffee tables and desks had been circulating in Microsoft's research group since the early 2000s, and Gates loved the idea. Gates believed that "surface computing," as he called it, was the wave of the future. Microsoft's Surface table didn't catch on, and eventually Microsoft stopped releasing the product. When Microsoft decided to make a new line of tablets to showcase its Windows 8 operating system, it decided to use the name "Surface" again.

HARDWARE FOR WINDOWS 8

In 2009, Microsoft programmers began working on Windows 8. The design of Windows 8 was heavily influenced by Apple's popular iPhone and its finger-friendly touch screen. In Windows 8, programmers got rid of the traditional Start menu and replaced it with what became popularly known as the Metro interface. The Metro interface consisted of large tiles that users could tap and push with their fingers.

Microsoft executives worried that traditional computer manufacturers would not make a touch screen computer that properly showcased its new operating system. "With Windows 8 we don't want to leave any seam uncovered; we wanted to give it its own hardware innovation," Ballmer said. "It's something new, something different, a whole new family of computing devices from Microsoft."[1]

Microsoft decided to enter the hardware market, creating the Surface tablet to fully highlight the capabilities of Windows 8. Microsoft's goal was to design an even better and more productive tablet than Apple's iPad, which came out in 2010. Microsoft designed the Surface to feel like a book. The tablet had a cover to protect its screen. On the back of the cover was a full keyboard. The Surface also had a built-in kickstand that helped it stand upright.

The first Surface tablet, however, could not run most existing Windows software. Instead, it ran a special version of Office and a few apps from the new Windows Store app market. In 2013, Microsoft released the Surface Pro. The Surface Pro had a higher resolution screen and a stylus pen for input, and it ran a full version of Windows 8.

A BALANCING ACT

Microsoft's Panos Panay led the team that created the first Surface tablet. "We needed to ensure it would happen right," Panay said.[2] It was tricky to build a tablet that had a keyboard in the front cover and a built-in kickstand in the back. To get the weight and feel of the tablet just right, Microsoft's design team made several prototype tablets using cardboard and tape.

Microsoft predicted it would sell two million Surface tablets in the last quarter of 2012 alone, but the company fell short of that mark. In March 2013, it was reported that Microsoft had only sold approximately 1.5 million Surface tablets.[3] Despite the poor performance of the Surface tablets, Microsoft stayed with the product, releasing the Surface 2 and Surface Pro 2 in late 2013. Again, sales were disappointing.

In 2014, Microsoft launched the Surface Pro 3, a thinner and lighter tablet with better performance than its predecessors. The Surface Pro 3 caught on with users, and Microsoft's Surface division posted its first profitable quarter at the end of September that year.

LAPTOP, TABLET, DRAWING PAD, AND PRESENTATION BOARD

The Surface Book was designed to operate in four different modes. It could function as a laptop with a full keyboard and an interactive touch screen. Users could also detach the interactive touch screen from the keyboard and use it as a tablet. The Surface Book could be folded on top of itself to work as a sketch pad with a stylus pen. Finally, it could also be used for presentations: users could detach the interactive screen, turn it around, and reattach the screen facing outward to an audience.

THE SURFACE BOOK AND STUDIO SURFACE

In 2015, Microsoft announced the Surface Book, the company's first traditional laptop. The Surface Book was heavier than the previous Surface tablets. It was designed to compete head-to-head with

Apple's MacBook Pro. Although the Surface Book was designed mainly as a laptop computer, users could press a button on the keyboard, detach the screen, and use the screen as a tablet.

Following the Surface Book, Microsoft launched its Surface Studio in 2016. The Surface Studio was designed as a desktop personal computer that could transform into a huge tablet for drawing. It had a vivid 28-inch (71 cm) touch screen for displaying text, videos, and pictures. The Surface Studio was intended for use by professional digital artists and designers.

THE SURFACE DIAL

The Surface Dial is an accessory for Microsoft's Surface Studio. It is a small, round device that sits on the Surface Studio's screen. An artist or designer can draw with one hand, while the other hand clicks and rotates the Surface Dial to bring up creative tools and shortcuts. The Dial was created to help artists stay in the flow of their work process. In an article for *Wired*, Elizabeth Stinson wrote, "If Surface Studio is your drafting table and the Surface Pen stylus is your pencil, then Dial is your palette. It's the object you hold in your other hand that contains all the tools you dip into on a regular basis."[4]

THE FUTURE OF SURFACE

The Surface line of products started out with very thin, lightweight tablets, but the future of Surface might lie with giant touch screen displays targeted for business users. In 2016, Microsoft shipped its first Surface

Hayete Gallot of Microsoft demonstrated the Surface Hub in 2015 at an event at the company's headquarters.

Hub computers to customers. The Surface Hub was a Windows 10 device with a giant 84-inch (213 cm) screen. The huge screen included microphones, cameras, and advanced sensors. It also had a digital whiteboard for writing and drawing. Users could hold video conference calls while writing on the whiteboard. Many large companies purchased Surface Hubs for their offices. It is the most popular Surface device for business users.

Microsoft announced the Surface Hub 2 in 2018. Its huge screen would be able to rotate to a portrait position. In an article for the *Verge*, Tom Warren described the Surface Hub 2 as the computer designed for the office of the future. He wrote, "Microsoft is working on a new dynamic collaboration scenario that will allow multiple people to walk up to the Surface Hub 2, log into the device using the built-in fingerprint reader and then each pull their own work into a single collaborative document. . . . far-field microphones and 4K cameras will allow you to make video calls in portrait mode that make it feel like you're standing next to a colleague."[5]

CHAPTER NINE

THE MICROSOFT OF THE FUTURE

S atya Nadella became Microsoft's new CEO in 2014. As Microsoft officially pulled out of the smartphone business in 2017, Nadella said that going forward Microsoft would focus on offering cloud computing services through its Azure platform and developing new artificial intelligence technologies. In a letter to Microsoft's shareholders in 2017, Nadella wrote, "We have galvanized the company's efforts around AI both to power each of our product categories with breakthrough capabilities and make the same capabilities available to our customers through Azure."[1]

Under Nadella's leadership, Microsoft is committed to "democratizing" artificial intelligence. This means Microsoft will give developers access to cloud computing services and software so they can create new artificial

Nadella began working at Microsoft in 1992 and rose to the level of CEO in 2014.

intelligence technologies. Nadella said Microsoft wants to make artificial intelligence technologies useful for everyday people.

CLOUD COMPUTING

Cloud computing happens when an individual or a business purchases computing services and accesses these services over the internet. For example, when people log onto the internet and access an email account, they are using cloud computing. Some cloud computing services are designed for individuals who want to store photos, documents, and videos, whereas other services focus on business users.

Cloud computing allows businesses to purchase the computing resources and services they need as they go along without having to buy and maintain expensive computer hardware and software in-house. It is similar to purchasing electricity or water from a utility company and then receiving a monthly bill for the amount of electricity or water used. Because cloud computing services are provided over the internet, people can access these services at any time and from anywhere around the world.

Cloud computing platforms rely on centralized collections of servers that store and process customers' data.

Microsoft offers cloud computing services through a platform called Azure. Azure includes a worldwide network of data centers that are regularly updated with the fastest and most efficient hardware. Microsoft offers three types of cloud computing services: infrastructure as a service (IaaS), platform as a service (PaaS), and software as a service (SaaS).

With IaaS, companies rent servers and virtual machines, storage, networking, and operating systems from Microsoft. With PaaS, companies purchase access to computing services that allow them to develop, test, and manage software applications. PaaS makes it easier for developers to create new apps because they don't have to buy the underlying computer equipment needed for development. With SaaS, companies can purchase the use of software applications such as Office 365 over the internet. Users can connect to the software application over the internet with a web browser from their personal computer, tablet, or smartphone.

Microsoft's competitors in the cloud computing market include Apple, Google, IBM, and Amazon. Although Microsoft was slow to respond to the mobile revolution, the company is determined to stake out a strong position in the cloud computing market.

BUILDING INTELLIGENT MACHINES

In 1991, Gates predicted that someday computers would see, hear, and learn just as humans do. Microsoft is working on turning this prediction into a reality. The company is infusing intelligence capabilities into its products, including Skype, Office 365, Cortana, and Bing. For example, Cortana can answer questions and retrieve information for users. Getting computers to understand natural spoken language is a significant challenge. Computers typically follow strict logical rules, but human speech can often be ambiguous or fail to follow correct grammar. Natural language processing breaks apart human speech and tries to figure out not only the words that were said but also their context. This makes it possible to deliver the response the user is looking for.

In 2016, Microsoft debuted another artificial intelligence program it had developed, Xiaoice. Xiaoice appeared on a Chinese morning news show and delivered the weather forecast. The bot also answered a question from the news anchor. Like Cortana, Xiaoice can answer questions, but Xiaoice is also programmed to detect human emotions and to remember conversations. Xiaoice's average conversation includes 26 turns between the user and the bot. Although Microsoft has not developed an English-speaking equivalent to Xiaoice, the creation of the intelligent bot is one example of how the company is creating computer programs that can interact with and assist humans.

MICROSOFT RENOVATES ITS REDMOND CAMPUS

In 2017, Microsoft announced a major renovation at its campus in Redmond. The Redmond campus serves as Microsoft's global headquarters. The renovation will include 18 new buildings, public transportation, and public spaces. There will be a plaza that will hold up to 12,000 people, sports fields, retail stores, and hiking trails. The company wants to make the campus as walking and biking friendly as possible. The goal of the project is to create an urban, city-like feel within the campus's forested setting. The renovation will take five to seven years to complete.

Microsoft also announced it was redeveloping its campus in Mountain View, California, in 2017. The redevelopment will incorporate environmentally friendly features, including a green roof that has plant species suitable to the area's local habitat. The buildings will be encased in glass to take advantage of natural light in employees' work areas. The campus will also include a water management system that will capture and reuse rainwater.

In 2018, Microsoft researchers reached another milestone in artificial intelligence technology. They created the first machine translation system that can translate sentences of news articles from Chinese to English with the same accuracy as a human translator. Researchers have worked for decades on developing a machine that could translate language as accurately as a human translator, and some experts believed it could not be done.

Three research teams in Microsoft's Beijing, China, and Redmond, Washington, labs worked together to create the machine. To develop the machine's intelligence, they taught the machine to go over its translations again and again to improve its responses. In essence, the machine would learn from its own mistakes and improve its translations over time.

By investing heavily in artificial intelligence technologies, Microsoft is positioning itself to be a leader in the future of computing. Nadella acknowledges that some people might be skeptical about Microsoft's ability to lead the next computing revolution. "To those of you who say, 'Well, is Microsoft capable?'—when you look at what we're doing with HoloLens on one side, and what we see as the future of mixed reality, what we're doing at our data centers every day at this scale . . . we have high ambition on a lot of these projects."[2]

SEEKING DIVERSITY

Like many tech companies, Microsoft has a workforce that is demographically very different from the nation as a whole. Women, African Americans, and Hispanics are all underrepresented in the company. Tech company leaders sometimes explain this by saying that people in these groups are also underrepresented in the hiring pool.

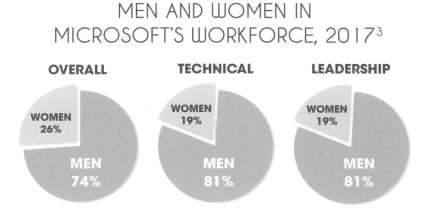

MEN AND WOMEN IN MICROSOFT'S WORKFORCE, 2017[3]

OVERALL

WOMEN 26%

MEN 74%

TECHNICAL

WOMEN 19%

MEN 81%

LEADERSHIP

WOMEN 19%

MEN 81%

Overall, Microsoft's workforce has a disproportionately small number of women compared to the general population. The gap widens when it comes to technical and leadership roles.

They say the issue is not that hiring managers pass over underrepresented groups but rather that these people are not applying for the jobs in the first place.

Whatever the reason for underrepresentation, Microsoft has taken steps to be more transparent and clear about its diversity goals. It describes diversity as a key part of its overall corporate vision. Its website discusses the ways in which it supports and invests in computer science education for young women and people of color. And the company releases statistics about the demographic makeup of its workforce to show where it has made progress and where it still wants to improve.

THE GLOBAL IMPACT OF MICROSOFT

Microsoft's products are at the center of people's daily lives. Its Windows operating system is found on personal computers around the world. People send emails, write documents, and create spreadsheets using tools in Microsoft's Office suite. Gamers can join in a worldwide online gaming community using Xbox Live. New technologies such as Microsoft's HoloLens are reimagining the way medical students learn anatomy or the way people view a dance performance. And it all

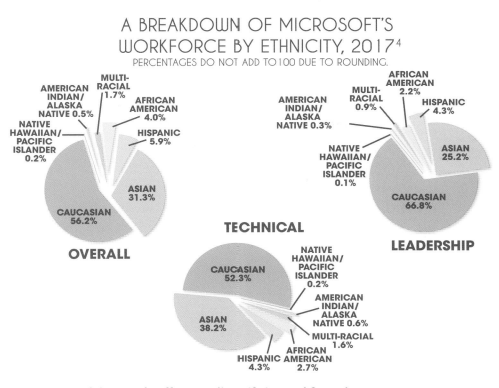

A BREAKDOWN OF MICROSOFT'S WORKFORCE BY ETHNICITY, 2017[4]

PERCENTAGES DO NOT ADD TO 100 DUE TO ROUNDING.

OVERALL

MULTI-RACIAL 1.7%
AMERICAN INDIAN/ALASKA NATIVE 0.5%
NATIVE HAWAIIAN/PACIFIC ISLANDER 0.2%
AFRICAN AMERICAN 4.0%
HISPANIC 5.9%
ASIAN 31.3%
CAUCASIAN 56.2%

TECHNICAL

CAUCASIAN 52.3%
ASIAN 38.2%
HISPANIC 4.3%
AFRICAN AMERICAN 2.7%
MULTI-RACIAL 1.6%
AMERICAN INDIAN/ALASKA NATIVE 0.6%
NATIVE HAWAIIAN/PACIFIC ISLANDER 0.2%

LEADERSHIP

AFRICAN AMERICAN 2.2%
MULTI-RACIAL 0.9%
HISPANIC 4.3%
AMERICAN INDIAN/ALASKA NATIVE 0.3%
NATIVE HAWAIIAN/PACIFIC ISLANDER 0.1%
ASIAN 25.2%
CAUCASIAN 66.8%

Microsoft has made efforts to diversify its workforce, but some groups remain underrepresented compared to the general population.

started with two young men who dreamed of putting a personal computer on every desk and in every home. As they strove to achieve this dream, Gates and Allen created one of the most successful computer companies in history and changed the way people live and work across the globe.

TIMELINE

1975
In April, Gates and Allen cofound Microsoft.

1979
In January, Microsoft moves from Albuquerque, New Mexico, to Bellevue, Washington.

1981
In August, IBM introduces its personal computer with Microsoft's operating system, MS-DOS.

1986
In February, Microsoft moves its corporate campus to Redmond, Washington; in March, Microsoft's stock goes public.

1989
In August, Microsoft introduces its earliest version of its Office suite of productivity applications.

1998
The Department of Justice files an antitrust lawsuit against Microsoft.

2000
In January, Ballmer is named president and CEO of Microsoft; Gates stays on as the company's chief software architect.

2001
Microsoft launches the Xbox.

2005
Microsoft launches the Xbox 360.

2008
Gates transitions from his day-to-day role at Microsoft to focus on his work at the Bill & Melinda Gates Foundation.

2009

Microsoft launches its Bing search engine.

2010

Microsoft releases Windows Phone.

2012

Microsoft launches Microsoft Surface.

2013

Microsoft launches the Xbox One.

2014

Satya Nadella is named the CEO of Microsoft; Microsoft completes its acquisition of the Nokia Devices and Services business.

2015

Microsoft launches Windows 10.

2016

Microsoft announces the formation of its new Artificial Intelligence and Research Group.

2017

Microsoft launches the Xbox One X; in November, the company announces a major Redmond campus renovation.

ESSENTIAL **FACTS**

FOUNDERS

- Bill Gates, Paul Allen

CEOs

- Bill Gates (1975–2000)

- Steve Ballmer (2000–2014)

- Satya Nadella (from 2014)

KEY STATISTICS

- Microsoft's Windows 10 operating system is active on more than 500 million devices around the world.

- More than 100 million people use Microsoft's Office 365 commercial software, and 27 million consumers use Office 365 Home & Personal software.

- In gaming, there are more than 53 million members active on Xbox Live.

- In 2017, Microsoft reported $89.5 billion in revenue. The company employs 128,290 people worldwide. Of those employees, 75,910 live in the United States. In the state of Washington alone, Microsoft has 47,679 employees.

IMPACT ON HISTORY

In Microsoft's more than 40 years, the company has made a name for itself by creating technologies that change the way people live and work. Microsoft's creation of its Windows operating system and its Microsoft Office suite set industry standards and helped popularize personal computers in homes and offices in the 1990s. The company has also influenced the video game industry with its line of Xbox consoles, and today it is making developments in new computer hardware and in cloud computing services.

QUOTE

"Microsoft arguably touches more lives on a daily basis than any other corporation on Earth."

—*Paul Allen*

GLOSSARY

clone

A computer that functions exactly like another more well-known computer.

code

A set of instructions in a computer program.

conservative

Conforming to traditional attitudes and values and cautious about innovation.

flop

A failure.

graphical user interface

A visual way of interacting with a computer using menus, icons, and windows.

hardware

The physical parts of the computer, including the keyboard and monitor, and also parts inside the computer, such as the hard drive and memory.

hologram

A three-dimensional image created by the interference of light from a laser or another light source.

microcomputer

A small computer, such as a personal computer.

morale

The emotional condition of an individual or a group.

operating system

The basic software on a computer that allows other software programs to work with the computer's hardware.

replica

An exact copy of something.

revenue

A company's income.

software

Various kinds of programs used to operate a computer.

stock

A piece of ownership in a company. When a person buys "stock," he or she buys a little piece (called a "share") of ownership in a company.

ADDITIONAL **RESOURCES**

SELECTED BIBLIOGRAPHY

Allen, Paul. *Idea Man: A Memoir by the Co-Founder of Microsoft.* Portfolio, 2010.

Mintz, Jessica. "Why Microsoft Embraced Gaming." *MIT Technology Review*, 3 Nov. 2013, technologyreview.com. Accessed 6 Aug. 2018.

Wallace, James, and Jim Erickson. *Hard Drive: Bill Gates and the Making of the Microsoft Empire.* John Wiley, 1992.

FURTHER READINGS

Cummings, Judy Dodge. *Apple.* Abdo, 2019.

Naber, Therese. *How the Computer Changed History.* Abdo, 2016.

ONLINE RESOURCES

Booklinks
NONFICTION NETWORK
FREE! ONLINE NONFICTION RESOURCES

To learn more about Microsoft, visit abdobooklinks.com. These links are routinely monitored and updated to provide the most current information available.

MORE INFORMATION

For more information on this subject, contact or visit the following organizations:

COMPUTER HISTORY MUSEUM

1401 N. Shoreline Blvd.

Mountain View, CA 94043

650-810-1010

computerhistory.org

The Computer History Museum features exhibits from throughout the history of the computer era. Included are many Microsoft products.

MICROSOFT VISITOR CENTER

15010 NE 36th St.

Microsoft Campus

Building 92

Redmond, WA 98052

425-703-6214

microsoft.com/en-us/visitorcenter

Visitors to Microsoft's visitor center can explore hands-on exhibits and learn about Microsoft's latest technologies.

SOURCE **NOTES**

CHAPTER 1. PIONEERING MIXED-REALITY TECHNOLOGY

1. Nina Strochlic. "Scientists Are Turning Your Body into Holograms." *National Geographic*, June 2017, nationalgeographic.com. Accessed 7 Aug. 2018.

2. "Microsoft Annual Report 2017." *Microsoft*, 16 Oct. 2017, microsoft.com. Accessed 7 Aug. 2018.

3. "Facts about Microsoft." *Microsoft*, n.d., news.microsoft.com. Accessed 7 Aug. 2018.

4. Leo Sun. "Microsoft Sells 'Thousands' of HoloLens—What Now?" *Motley Fool*, 2 Feb. 2017, fool.com. Accessed 7 Aug. 2018.

5. Will Greenwald. "Microsoft HoloLens Development Edition." *PCMAG*, 22 Aug. 2016, pcmag.com. Accessed 7 Aug. 2018.

6. "CWRU, Cleveland Clinic Collaborate with Microsoft on Mixed-Reality Technology." *Daily*, 30 Apr. 2015, thedaily.case.edu. Accessed 7 Aug. 2018.

7. "CWRU Takes the Stage at Microsoft's Build Conference to Show How HoloLens Can Transform Learning." *Daily*, 31 Mar. 2016, thedaily.case.edu. Accessed 7 Aug. 2018.

8. Strochlic, "Scientists Are Turning Your Body into Holograms."

9. "HoloAnatomy App Earns Another Top Honor." *Daily*, 15 Dec. 2016, thedaily. case.edu. Accessed 7 Aug. 2018.

10. "NASA, Microsoft Collaboration Will Allow Scientists to 'Work on Mars.'" *NASA*, 21 Jan. 2015, jpl.nasa.gov. Accessed 7 Aug. 2018.

11. Alan Boyle. "Microsoft's HoloLens Headset Wins Rave Review from Astronaut Scott Kelly after Year in Space." *GeekWire*, 5 Mar. 2016, geekwire.com. Accessed 7 Aug. 2018.

12. Satya Nadella. "Annual Report 2017." *Microsoft*, 2017, microsoft.com. Accessed 7 Aug. 2018.

CHAPTER 2. MICROSOFT IS BORN

1. Paul Allen. *Idea Man: A Memoir by the Co-Founder of Microsoft*. Portfolio, 2012. 6–7.

2. Allen, *Idea Man*, 7.

3. Steven Levy. "Power to the People." *Newsweek*, 24 Sept. 2007, newsweek.com. Accessed 7 Aug. 2018.

4. James Wallace and Jim Erickson. *Hard Drive: Bill Gates and the Making of the Microsoft Empire*. John Wiley, 1993. 76–77.

5. Wallace and Erickson, *Hard Drive*, 92.

6. Levy, "Power to the People."

7. Wallace and Erickson, *Hard Drive*, 7.

8. "Timeline: Bill Gates." *NPR*, June 2008, npr.org. Accessed 7 Aug. 2018.

9. Wallace and Erickson, *Hard Drive*, 109–110.

CHAPTER 3. THE IBM DEAL

1. James Wallace and Jim Erickson. *Hard Drive: Bill Gates and the Making of the Microsoft Empire*. John Wiley, 1993. 204.

2. Wallace and Erickson, *Hard Drive*, 170.

3. Wallace and Erickson, *Hard Drive*, 141.

4. Wallace and Erickson, *Hard Drive*, 141.

5. Wallace and Erickson, *Hard Drive*, 169.

6. Paul Andrews. "How IBM's PC Made Microsoft." *US News & World Report*, 20 Aug. 2001, usnews.com. Accessed 7 Aug 2018.

7. Paul Allen, *Idea Man: A Memoir by the Co-Founder of Microsoft*. Portfolio, 2012. 25.

8. "Paul Allen Fast Facts." *CNN*, 8 Mar. 2018, cnn.com. Accessed 7 Aug. 2018.

9. "Paul Allen." *Biography*, 27 Mar. 2018, biography.com. Accessed 7 Aug. 2018.

10. "Paul Allen Fast Facts."

11. Andrews, "How IBM's PC Made Microsoft."

12. Lincoln Spector. "The PC at 20." *PC World*, Aug. 2001, pcworld.com. Accessed 7 Aug. 2018.

13. Andrews, "How IBM's PC Made Microsoft."

14. Wallace and Erickson, *Hard Drive*, 215.

15. Andrews, "How IBM's PC Made Microsoft."

16. Wallace and Erickson, *Hard Drive*, 187.

17. Andrews, "How IBM's PC Made Microsoft."

CHAPTER 4. THE BIRTH OF WINDOWS

1. Paul Allen. *Idea Man: A Memoir by the Co-Founder of Microsoft*. Portfolio, 2012. 139–140.

2. James Wallace and Jim Erickson. *Hard Drive: Bill Gates and the Making of the Microsoft Empire*. John Wiley, 1993. 251.

3. Wallace and Erickson, *Hard Drive*, 313.

4. Wallace and Erickson, *Hard Drive*, 362.

5. Wallace and Erickson, *Hard Drive*, 362.

6. Wallace and Erickson, *Hard Drive*, 361.

7. Wayne Rash. "Windows at 30: How Microsoft Changed the Personal Computing World." *EWeek*, 21 Nov. 2015, eweek.com. Accessed 7 Aug. 2018.

8. Allen, *Idea Man*, 181.

9. Wallace Chu. "Microsoft Office through the Years." *Smart Buyer*, 3 Nov. 2016, neweggbusiness.com. Accessed 7 Aug. 2018.

10. Andre Da Costa. "A Look at 25 Years of Microsoft Then and Now." *Groovypost*, 20 Apr. 2018, groovypost.com. Accessed 7 Aug. 2018.

11. Wallace and Erickson, *Hard Drive*, 330.

12. Allen, *Idea Man*, 191.

CHAPTER 5. THE INTERNET REVOLUTION

1. Paul Allen, *Idea Man: A Memoir by the Co-Founder of Microsoft*. Portfolio, 2012. 176.

2. "May 26, 1995: Gates, Microsoft Jump on 'Internet Tidal Wave.'" *Wired*, 4 June 2017, wired.com. Accessed 7 Aug. 2018.

3. "May 26, 1995."

SOURCE **NOTES**
CONTINUED

4. James Wallace and Jim Erickson. *Hard Drive: Bill Gates and the Making of the Microsoft Empire*. John Wiley, 1993. 374–375.

5. "May 26, 1995."

6. "May 26, 1995."

7. "May 26, 1995."

8. Don Reisinger. "10 Milestones in Internet Explorer's Storied History." *Eweek*, 14 Jan. 2016, eweek.com. Accessed 7 Aug. 2018.

9. "Why Bill Gates Should Worry." *Economist*, 20 Dec. 1997, economist.com. Accessed 7 Aug. 2018.

10. Charles Arthur. *Digital Wars: Apple, Google, Microsoft, and the Battle for the Internet*. KoganPage, 2014. 3.

11. Erik Gregersen. "Bing." *Encyclopedia Britannica*, 17 Nov. 2017, britannica.com. Accessed 7 Aug. 2018.

12. Tom McNichol. "Can Microsoft's Bing Take a Bite Out of Google?" *Time*, 31 July 2009, content.time.com. Accessed 7 Aug. 2018.

13. "Share of Search Queries by Leading US Search Engine Providers as of January 2018." *Statista*, Jan. 2018, statista.com. Accessed 7 Aug. 2018.

CHAPTER 6. MICROSOFT ENTERS GAMING

1. Rick Marshall. "The History of the Xbox." *Digital Trends*, 12 May 2013, digitaltrends.com. Accessed 7 Aug. 2018.

2. Marshall, "The History of the Xbox."

3. Derek Strickland. "Xbox LIVE Monthly Active Users Up 13% to 53 Million." *TweakTown*, 27 Oct. 2017, tweaktown.com. Accessed 7 Aug. 2018.

4. Marshall, "The History of the Xbox."

5. Marshall, "The History of the Xbox."

6. Marshall, "The History of the Xbox."

7. Marshall, "The History of the Xbox."

8. Andrew Webster. "Microsoft Announces the Xbox One S, Its Smallest Xbox Yet." *Verge*, 13 June 2016, theverge.com. Accessed 7 Aug. 2018.

9. Kyle Orland. "Reports: PS4 Is Selling Twice as Well as Xbox One, Overall." *Ars Technica*, 18 Jan. 2017, arstechnica.com. Accessed 7 Aug. 2018.

10. Patrick Goss. "Ten Years of Xbox: A Brief History." *TechRadar*, 15 Nov. 2011, techradar.com. Accessed 7 Aug. 2018.

11. Will Greenwald. "Microsoft Xbox One X." *PCMAG*, 3 Nov. 2017, pcmag.com. Accessed 7 Aug. 2018.

12. Jose Pagliery. "Microsoft Buys Minecraft Video Game Maker for $2.5 Billion." *CNN Money*, 15 Sept. 2014, money.cnn.com. Accessed 7 Aug. 2018.

13. Pagliery, "Microsoft Buys Minecraft Video Game Maker."

CHAPTER 7. GOING MOBILE

1. Adam Pothitos. "The History of the Smartphone." *Mobile Industry Review*, 31 Oct. 2016, mobileindustryreview.com. Accessed 7 Aug. 2018.

2. Charles Arthur. *Digital Wars: Apple, Google, Microsoft, and the Battle for the Internet*. KoganPage, 2014. 216.

3. Charles Arthur. "The History of Smartphones: Timeline." *Guardian*, 24 Jan. 2012, theguardian.com. Accessed 7 Aug. 2018.

4. Arthur, *Digital Wars*, 9.

5. Steve Brachmann. "A Brief History of Smartphones." *IPWatchdog*, 3 Mar. 2017, ipwatchdog.com. Accessed 7 Aug. 2018.

6. Brachmann, "A Brief History of Smartphones."

7. Taylor Martin. "Pocket Computing: Evolution of the Smartphone." *Pocketnow*, 29 July 2014, pocketnow.com. Accessed 7 Aug. 2018.

8. Brian X. Chen. "How Microsoft Blew It with Windows Mobile." *Wired*, 4 June 2017, wired.com. Accessed 7 Aug. 2018.

9. Arthur, "The History of Smartphones: Timeline."

10. Tom Warren. "Microsoft Morphs into a Hardware Giant with Closure of Nokia Deal." *Verge*, 25 Apr. 2014, theverge.com. Accessed 7 Aug. 2018.

11. Mary Jo Foley. "Microsoft Is Now Your 'Devices and Services' Company." *CNET*, 9 Oct. 2012, cnet.com. Accessed 7 Aug. 2018.

12. Vlad Savov. "Windows Phone Was a Glorious Failure." *Verge*, 10 Oct. 2017, theverge.com. Accessed 7 Aug. 2018.

CHAPTER 8. MICROSOFT SURFACE

1. Mark Sullivan. "Microsoft Announces Surface Tablet PC." *PC World*, 18 June 2012, pcworld.com. Accessed 7 Aug. 2018.

2. Matt Weinberger. "How Microsoft Built a Computer So Good, Even Apple Wanted to Copy It." *Business Insider*, 21 Aug. 2016, businessinsider.com. Accessed 7 Aug. 2018.

3. Weinberger, "How Microsoft Built a Computer."

4. Elizabeth Stinson. "You Might Not Need Surface Dial, But You're Probably Going to Want It." *Wired*, 3 June 2017, wired.com. Accessed 7 Aug. 2018.

5. Tom Warren. "Microsoft's Surface Hub 2 Is Designed for an Office of the Future." *Verge*, 15 May 2018, theverge.com. Accessed 7 Aug. 2018.

CHAPTER 9. THE MICROSOFT OF THE FUTURE

1. "Microsoft Annual Report 2017." *Microsoft*, 16 Oct. 2017, microsoft.com. Accessed 7 Aug. 2018.

2. Todd Bishop. "Microsoft's Quantum Future: Satya Nadella Gives Company Alums a Glimpse of What's Coming." *GeekWire*, 16 Aug. 2017, geekwire.com. Accessed 7 Aug. 2018.

3. "Inside Microsoft." *Microsoft*, 1 Sept. 2017, microsoft.com. Accessed 7 Aug. 2018.

4. "Inside Microsoft."

INDEX

ABOUT THE **AUTHOR**

LAURA LANE

Laura Lane grew up in Denver, Colorado. She attended the University of Colorado and earned degrees in English and law. After her daughter and son were born, she decided to pursue her dream of writing books for children. She and her husband, two children, and two cats now live in Madison, Wisconsin.

ABOUT THE **CONSULTANT**

ANTHONY ROTOLO

Anthony Rotolo was a college professor for more than ten years, teaching at Syracuse University. He taught courses in technology and media, including the very first college class on social media. He is now studying for a PhD in psychology and researching how social media affects people and society.